31 Easy Vegetarian BBQ Recipes

One Month of Easy, Meat Free Grilling

Mary Scott

Disclaimer

Copyright © 2015 by Mary Scott, Wings of Eagles Publications, LLC.

All rights Reserved. No part of this publication or the information in it may be quoted from or reproduced in any form by means such as printing, scanning, photocopying or otherwise without prior written permission of the copyright holder.

Disclaimer and Terms of Use: Effort has been made to ensure that the information in this book is accurate and complete, however, the author and the publisher do not warrant the accuracy of the information, text and graphics contained within the book due to the rapidly changing nature of science, research, known and unknown facts and internet. The Author and the publisher do not hold any responsibility for errors, omissions or contrary interpretation of the subject matter herein. This book is presented solely for motivational and informational purposes only.

The recipes and information provided in this report are for educational purposes only and are not intended to provide dietary advice. Readers are strongly encouraged to consult a doctor before making the dietary changes that are required when switching to a Vegetarian lifestyle. Recipe directions are provided as a guideline only as the quality of kitchen appliances varies and could result in the need for longer or shorter cooking times. All precautions should be taken to ensure food is fully cooked in order to prevent risk of foodborne illnesses. The author and publisher do not take responsibility for any consequences that are believed to be a result of following the instructions in this book.

All rights reserved.

Grilled Romaine Blue Cheese Salad 36

Honey-Dipped Grilled Artichokes 38

Garlic Asiago Grilled Asparagus 40

Grilled Avocado with Tomato Salsa 41

BBQ Stuffed Sweet Peppers 43

Balsamic-Grilled Vegetable Medley 44

Chipotle Grilled Sweet Potatoes 45

Grilled Polenta Cakes with Mango Salsa 46

Grilled Barbecue Seitan Ribs 48

Smoked Seitan "Brisket" 50

Conclusion 52

Introduction

Numerous studies have shown the health benefits associated with a vegetarian diet. According to Dr. Rachel K. Johnson, meat and animal fats are high in the type of saturated fats that can lead to an increased risk for heart disease in women. On the other hand, a vegetarian diet is very low in saturated fats which means that it may help you to lower your cholesterol levels as well as your risk for heart disease. In addition to being low in saturated fat, the vegetarian diet is also often lower in calories than the standard American diet. Multiple research studies, including one called the European Prospective Investigation in Cancer and Nutrition Oxford study, showed that vegetarians (especially vegans) have consistently lower body mass indexes (BMI) than meat-eaters. Over a 5-year study of nearly 22,000 men and women, weight gain was the lowest among those following a plant-based diet.

Not only does the vegetarian diet reduce your risk for heart disease and have the potential to help you lose weight, but it may also help you to stave off certain types of cancer. In 2007, the World Cancer Research Fund reported that consumption of red meats and processed meats could raise your risk for colorectal cancer. It may be the increased fiber content of the vegetarian diet which helps to prevent this particular type of cancer. Other studies have found that vegetarian foods contain a variety of protective compounds which help to prevent the initiation of cancer while also retarding the growth of cancer cells. Vegetarians and vegans have also been known to experience benefits in terms of preventing or managing other chronic diseases like hypertension, diabetes, and rheumatoid arthritis.

If the health benefits associated with the vegetarian diet are not enough to convince you of its merit, consider the fact that many vegetarian dishes are loaded with flavor. Just because you give up meat doesn't mean that you have to say goodbye to all of your favorite dishes. There are plenty of meat-free alternatives for popular dishes including pizza, burgers, pasta dishes, and even barbecue. This book is dedicated to satisfying your cravings for some good old-fashioned barbecue. In this book you will find a collection of 31 delicious vegetarian barbecue recipes including everything from grilled pizza and burgers to kebabs, sandwiches, and more. Say goodbye to boring vegetarian dishes and bite into one of these tasty BBQ options – you won't be disappointed!

Grilled Pesto Mozzarella Pizza

Servings: 6

Pesto Ingredients:

- 2 cups fresh basil, packed
- ¼ cup plus 2 tablespoons pine nuts
- ½ cup fresh grated parmesan cheese
- 1 tablespoon minced garlic
- ½ cup extra-virgin olive oil

Pizza Ingredients:

- 1 lbs. fresh pizza dough (if frozen, thawed)
- Olive oil, as needed
- ½ small red onion, sliced thin
- 2 to 3 ounces fresh mozzarella, sliced thin

Instructions:

1. Combine the basil and pine nuts in a food processor, pulsing to combine.
2. Blend in the garlic and parmesan cheese until smooth.
3. With the processor running, drizzle in the oil – season with salt and pepper to taste.
4. To prepare the pizza, preheat your grill to medium-high heat.
5. Divide the pizza dough in half and spread each half into a 10-inch circle.
6. Place the dough circles on a baking sheet then brush the tops with oil.
7. Place the pizza dough circles oil-side down on the grill – cook (with the grill closed) for 2 minutes until the bottom is crisp.
8. Brush the top of the dough circles with oil and flip them over – grill 2 minutes more until crisp.

9. Spread a few tablespoons of fresh pesto over the tops of the pizzas and top with slices of onion and mozzarella to serve.

Nutritional Information:

530 calories per serving, 39g fat, 37g carbs, 11g protein, 4g fiber, 3g sugar

BBQ Eggplant Parmesan Pizza

Servings: 6

Ingredients:

- 1 lbs. fresh pizza dough (if frozen, thawed)
- Olive oil, as needed
- 1 lbs. eggplant, sliced very thin
- Salt and pepper to taste
- 1 lbs. fresh tomatoes, sliced thin
- 1 cup crumbled goat cheese
- ½ cup fresh basil leaves, chopped

Instructions:

1. Preheat your grill to medium-high heat.
2. Divide the pizza dough in half and spread each half into a 10-inch circle.
3. Place the dough circles on a baking sheet then brush the tops with oil – set aside.
4. Brush the eggplant with olive oil and season with salt and pepper to taste.
5. Place the slices of eggplant on the grill, cooking for 3 to 4 minutes on each side with the grill cover closed.
6. Remove the eggplant to a plate to keep warm.
7. Place the pizza dough circles oil-side down on the grill – cook (with the grill closed) for 2 minutes until the bottom is crisp.
8. Brush the top of the dough circles with oil and flip them over – grill 2 minutes more until crisp.
9. Remove the dough circles to the baking sheet and top with slices of eggplant and tomatoes.
10. Sprinkle with fresh basil and goat cheese then serve immediately.

Nutritional Information:

510 calories per serving, 35g fat, 40g carbs, 11.5g protein, 6g fiber, 5g sugar

Grilled Red Pepper and Zucchini Pizza

Servings: 6

Ingredients:

- 1 lbs. fresh pizza dough (if frozen, thawed)
- Olive oil, as needed
- 2 small zucchini, sliced very thin
- ¼ teaspoon onion powder
- 1 to 2 tablespoons minced garlic
- ½ cup roasted red pepper in oil, drained and chopped
- 1 cup crumbled feta cheese

Instructions:

1. Preheat your grill to medium-high heat.
2. Divide the pizza dough in half and spread each half into a 10-inch circle.
3. Place the dough circles on a baking sheet then brush the tops with oil.
4. Place the pizza dough circles oil-side down on the grill – cook (with the grill closed) for 2 minutes until the bottom is crisp.
5. Brush the top of the dough circles with oil and flip them over – grill 2 minutes more until crisp.
6. Remove the pizza crusts to the baking sheet and sprinkle the edges with onion powder.
7. Sprinkle the garlic over the pizza crusts along with the roasted red pepper.
8. Spread a piece of foil on the grill and spread the sliced zucchini over it.
9. Grill the zucchini for 2 to 3 minutes on each side until lightly charred.
10. Top the pizzas with slices of grilled zucchini and crumbled feta cheese to serve.

Nutritional Information:

480 calories per serving, 33g fat, 37g carbs, 8g protein, 3g fiber, 3g sugar

Crispy Grilled Margherita Pizza

Servings: 6

Pizza Ingredients:

- 1 lbs. fresh pizza dough (if frozen, thawed)
- Olive oil, as needed
- 1 large ripe tomato, sliced thin
- 2 to 3 ounces fresh mozzarella, sliced thin
- ¼ to 1/3 cup fresh basil leaves

Instructions:

1. Preheat your grill to medium-high heat.
2. Divide the pizza dough in half and spread each half into a 10-inch circle.
3. Place the dough circles on a baking sheet then brush the tops with oil.
4. Place the pizza dough circles oil-side down on the grill – cook (with the grill closed) for 2 minutes until the bottom is crisp.
5. Brush the top of the dough circles with oil and flip them over – grill 2 minutes more until crisp.
6. Remove the pizzas to the baking sheet.
7. Top the pizzas with slices of tomato and mozzarella – sprinkle with fresh basil to serve.

Nutritional Information:

450 calories per serving, 30g fat, 35g carbs, 9g protein, 3.5g fiber, 2g sugar

Grilled Sriracha Tofu Skewers

Servings: 4

Ingredients:

- 1 lbs. extra-firm tofu, cut into cubes
- 1 large zucchini, cut ¼-inch thick
- 1 red bell pepper, cored and cut into 1-inch chunks
- 10 large mushrooms, halved
- 1 small red onion, cut into wedges
- ½ cup soy sauce
- ¼ cup Sriracha sauce
- ¼ cup sesame oil
- 2 jalapenos, seeded and minced

Instructions:

1. Soak some wooden skewers in water for about 30 minutes.
2. Combine the tofu and vegetables in a large bowl.
3. Whisk together the soy sauce, Sriracha, sesame oil, and jalapeno in a separate bowl.
4. Toss the tofu and vegetables with the sauce to coat then chill for 1 hour.
5. Preheat the grill to medium heat and brush the grates with olive oil.
6. Thread the tofu and vegetables onto the skewer.
7. Place the skewers on the grill and cook for 10 to 12 minutes, turning occasionally, until the vegetables are tender.

Nutritional Information:

285 calories per serving, 21g fat, 13g carbs, 17g protein, 3.5g fiber, 6g sugar

Chimichurri Seitan Kebabs on the Grill

Servings: 8 to 10

Ingredients:

- 1 ½ lbs. seitan, cut into chunks
- 2 cups fresh chopped parsley
- 1/3 cup red wine vinegar
- 2 tablespoons minced garlic
- 2 tablespoons diced red onion
- ½ tablespoon fresh lemon juice
- 1 teaspoon red pepper flakes
- 1 teaspoon salt
- ½ cup plus 2 tablespoons olive oil

Instructions:

1. Soak some wooden skewers in water for about 30 minutes.
2. Combine the ingredients except for the seitan in a food processor.
3. Blend the mixture until smooth.
4. Spread the seitan in a shallow dish and pour in ¾ cups sauce – turn the seitan to coat then cover and chill for 2 to 4 hours.
5. Preheat the grill to medium heat and brush the grates with olive oil.
6. Slide the seitan pieces onto the skewers and place them on the grill.
7. Grill the 5 to 6 minutes on each side and serve with the rest of the sauce for dipping.

Nutritional Information:

130 calories per serving, 12g fat, 2g carbs, 4g protein, 1g fiber, 0g sugar

Grilled Greek Vegetable Kebabs

Servings: 6

Ingredients:

- 1 medium zucchini, sliced ¼-inch thick
- 1 yellow bell pepper, cored and cut into 1-inch chunks
- 1 red bell pepper, cored and cut into 1-inch chunks
- 2 cups cherry tomatoes
- 3 tablespoons olive oil
- 1 tablespoon fresh lemon juice
- ½ teaspoon dried oregano
- Salt and pepper to taste

Instructions:

1. Soak some wooden skewers in water for about 30 minutes.
2. Combine the vegetables in a bowl and toss with the olive oil, lemon juice, oregano, salt and pepper.
3. Preheat the grill to medium heat and brush the grates with olive oil.
4. Thread the vegetables onto the skewer.
5. Place the skewers on the grill and cook for 10 to 12 minutes, turning occasionally, until the vegetables are tender.

Nutritional Information:

90 calories per serving, 7g fat, 6g carbs, 1.5g protein, 2g fiber, 4g sugar

Indian-Spiced Veggie Skewers

Servings: 4

Ingredients:

- 2 small heads broccoli, cut into florets
- 1 small head cauliflower, cut into florets
- 1 ½ cups baby carrots
- 1 medium red onion, cut into wedges
- 2 large tomatoes, quartered
- 1/3 cup chickpea flour
- 1 cup plain yogurt
- ¼ cup fresh lemon juice
- ¼ cup olive oil
- 1 ½ tablespoons minced garlic
- 1 tablespoon fresh grated ginger
- 1 ½ teaspoon garam masala
- 1 ½ teaspoon paprika
- 1 teaspoon ground turmeric
- 1 teaspoon ground coriander

Instructions:

1. Soak some wooden skewers in water for about 30 minutes.
2. Bring a pot of salted water to boil then add the cauliflower, broccoli, and carrots.
3. Bring to a boil again then cook for 30 minutes.
4. Turn off the heat and drain the vegetables – rinse under cold water then pat dry.
5. Combine the remaining ingredients except the onion and tomatoes in a mixing bowl and toss in cooked vegetables with the onion and tomatoes.
6. Cover and chill for 30 minutes.

7. Preheat the grill to medium heat and brush the grates with olive oil.
8. Slide the vegetables onto the skewers then place them on the grill.
9. Cook for 1 minute then flip the skewers and cook for another minute or until done.

Nutritional Information:

290 calories per serving, 15g fat, 31g carbs, 11g protein, 9g fiber, 14g sugar

Grilled Satay Tempeh Kebabs

Servings: 6 to 8

Ingredients:

- 1 small yellow onion, chopped
- 1 teaspoon minced garlic
- 1 tablespoon minced ginger
- 1 stalk lemongrass, sliced
- ½ tablespoons Thai chile sauce
- 1 cup light coconut milk
- ½ tablespoon brown sugar
- ½ cup water
- 1 teaspoon lime zest
- 1 lbs. tempeh, cut into chunks or cubes

Instructions:

1. Soak some wooden skewers in water for about 30 minutes.
2. Combine the onion, garlic, ginger and lemon grass in a food processor – pulse to chop.
3. Add the chile sauce, coconut milk, brown sugar and water – pulse until well combined.
4. Transfer the mixture to a saucepan and stir in the lime zest.
5. Bring to a slow boil then toss in the tempeh.
6. Reduce heat to medium-low and simmer 20 minutes, covered, then remove from heat.
7. Preheat the grill to medium heat and brush the grates with olive oil.
8. Thread the tempeh onto the skewers and grill for 5 to 6 minutes on each side. Serve hot.

Nutritional Information:

270 calories per serving, 16g fat, 21g carbs, 14g protein, 10g fiber, 3g sugar

Mustard-Glazed Vegetable Kebabs

Servings: 4 to 6

Ingredients:

- Wooden skewers (soaked)
- 3 tablespoons olive oil
- 1 ½ tablespoons honey
- ½ tablespoon Dijon mustard
- 2 assorted bell peppers, cored and cut into 1-inch chunks
- 1 medium zucchini, cut into ½-inch slices
- 1 medium eggplant, cut into ½-inch slices
- 1 medium red onion, cut into wedges
- 12 cherry tomatoes

Instructions:

1. Soak some wooden skewers in water for about 30 minutes.
2. Preheat the grill to medium heat and brush the grates with olive oil.
3. Whisk together the olive oil, honey and mustard in a small bowl.
4. Slide the vegetables onto the skewers.
5. Place the skewers on the grill and cook for 15 to 20 minutes, turning occasionally and brushing with the mustard mixture.
6. Serve the skewers hot with the remaining glaze.

Nutritional Information:

165 calories per serving, 8g fat, 24g carbs, 4g protein, 7g fiber, 15g sugar

Grilled Portabella Burgers

Servings: 4

Ingredients:

- 2 tablespoons olive oil
- 2 teaspoons minced garlic
- Salt and pepper to taste
- 4 large Portobello mushroom caps, stems removed
- 4 sandwich buns, toasted

Instructions:

1. Preheat your grill to medium-high heat and brush the grates with olive oil.
2. Combine the olive oil, garlic, salt and pepper in a mixing bowl.
3. Brush the mixture over the mushrooms and place them on the grill.
4. Cook for 3 minutes per side until tender.
5. Serve the burgers hot on toasted sandwich buns with your favorite burger toppings.

Nutritional Information:

200 calories per serving, 9g fat, 26g carbs, 6g protein, 2g fiber, 4g sugar

Chickpea Veggie Burgers

Servings: 6

Ingredients:

- 4 tablespoons olive oil
- 1 tablespoon minced garlic
- 2 teaspoons ground cumin seed
- 2 (15-ounce) cans chickpeas, rinsed and drained
- 3 tablespoons tahini
- 1 tablespoon fresh lemon juice
- 1 large egg, beaten
- ½ cup plain breadcrumbs
- 3 tablespoons fresh chopped cilantro
- 6 sandwich buns, toasted

Instructions:

1. Preheat your grill to medium-high heat and brush the grates with olive oil.
2. Combine the oil, garlic and cumin in a small saucepan over medium-low heat.
3. Cook for 2 minutes until fragrant then remove from heat.
4. Combine 1 can of chickpeas with the garlic oil mixture in a food processor.
5. Add the tahini, lemon juice, and the egg – blend until smooth.
6. Pour in the rest of the chickpeas along with the breadcrumbs and cilantro.
7. Pulse until the mixture is well blended then season with salt and pepper to taste.
8. Shape the chickpea mixture by hand into 6 even-sized patties and brush with oil.

9. Grill the patties for about 2 to 3 minutes per side until heated through.
10. Serve hot on toasted sandwich buns with your favorite burger toppings.

Nutritional Information:

600 calories per serving, 19g fat, 87g carbs, 26g protein, 20g fiber, 14g sugar

Black Bean Veggie Burgers

Servings: 4

Ingredients:

- 2 (15-ounce) cans black beans, rinsed and drained
- 1 cup plain breadcrumbs
- ½ small white onion, diced
- 1 large egg, beaten
- 1 teaspoon chili powder
- 1 teaspoon hot sauce
- Salt and pepper to taste
- 4 sandwich buns, toasted

Instructions:

1. Preheat your grill to medium-high heat and brush the grates with olive oil.
2. Place the beans in a mixing bowl and gently mash them with a fork, leaving some beans mostly whole.
3. Stir in the remaining ingredients until well combined.
4. Let the mixture rest for 5 minutes then shape into four even-sized patties by hand.
5. Brush the patties with olive oil then place them on the grill.
6. Grill the patties for about 2 to 3 minutes per side until heated through.
7. Serve hot on toasted sandwich buns with your favorite burger toppings.

Nutritional Information:

615 calories per serving, 6g fat, 100g carbs, 32g protein, 19g fiber, 7g sugar

Eggplant Pesto Burgers

Servings: 4

Ingredients:

- 1 medium eggplant
- 1 tablespoon olive oil
- 1 tablespoon balsamic vinegar
- ¼ teaspoon dried oregano
- ¼ teaspoon dried basil
- Salt and pepper to taste
- 1/3 cup fresh basil pesto
- 4 sandwich buns, toasted
- 2 to 3 ounces fresh mozzarella cheese, sliced
- 1 large tomato, sliced

Instructions:

1. Slice the eggplant into four ½-inch slices at the widest part of the eggplant.
2. Combine the olive oil, balsamic vinegar, and herbs in a mixing bowl – season with salt and pepper to taste.
3. Place the eggplant rounds in a shallow dish and pour in the marinade.
4. Turn the slices to coat then let soak for 20 minutes.
5. Preheat your grill to medium-high heat and brush the grates with olive oil.
6. Place the eggplant slices on the grill.
7. Grill the slices for about 5 to 6 minutes per side until tender.
8. Spread the pesto on the toasted sandwich buns and add a slice of eggplant to each.
9. Top with slices of fresh mozzarella cheese and tomato.

Nutritional Information:

230 calories per serving, 8g fat, 30g carbs, 10g protein, 5.5g fiber, 7g sugar

Whole-Grain Pumpkin Burgers

Servings: 6

Ingredients:

- 2 cups chopped pumpkin, cooked
- 1 (15-ounce) can white beans, rinsed and drained
- 1 tablespoon chia seeds
- 1 tablespoon roasted minced garlic
- 1 teaspoon fresh chopped rosemary
- Salt and pepper to taste
- 1 cup quinoa, cooked and cooled
- ½ cup quinoa flour
- ½ cup plain breadcrumbs
- 1 small red onion, diced
- 4 sandwich buns, toasted

Instructions:

1. Combine the pumpkin, beans, chia seeds, garlic, and rosemary in a food processor.
2. Pulse several times then blend smooth – season with salt and pepper to taste.
3. Transfer the mixture to a mixing bowl and stir in the quinoa, quinoa flour, breadcrumbs and red onion.
4. Freeze for 30 minutes then divide into 6 even-sized patties by hand.
5. Preheat your grill to medium-high heat and brush the grates with olive oil.
6. Place the patties on the grill and cook for 4 to 5 minutes on each side until cooked through.
7. Serve hot on toasted sandwich buns with your favorite burger toppings.

Nutritional Information:

560 calories per serving, 7g fat, 94g carbs, 30g protein, 18g fiber, 7g sugar

Sweet Potato Kale Burgers

Servings: 4

Ingredients:

- ¾ cups water
- 1/3 cup uncooked quinoa, rinsed well
- 1 medium sweet potato, baked and cooled
- 6 leaves kale, stems removed and chopped
- 1 teaspoon minced garlic
- 1 teaspoon fresh lemon juice
- Salt and pepper to taste
- 4 sandwich buns, toasted

Instructions:

1. Bring the water and quinoa to boil in a saucepan with a pinch of salt.
2. Reduce heat and simmer, covered, for 10 minutes then turn off heat.
3. Spoon the sweet potatoes into a mixing bowl and mash with a potato masher.
4. Stir in the kale along with the quinoa and garlic.
5. Add the lemon juice and season with salt and pepper to taste – stir until well combined.
6. Preheat your grill to medium-high heat and brush the grates with olive oil.
7. Divide the mixture into four even-sized patties by hand and brush with olive oil.
8. Place the patties on the grill and cook for 4 to 5 minutes on each side until cooked through.
9. Serve hot on toasted sandwich buns with your favorite burger toppings.

Nutritional Information:

220 calories per serving, 3g fat, 40g carbs, 8g protein, 3.5g fiber, 5g sugar

White Bean and Quinoa Burgers

Servings: 4

Ingredients:

- 1 cup water
- ½ cup uncooked quinoa, rinsed well
- 1 (15-ounce) can white beans, rinsed and drained
- ½ cup frozen corn, thawed
- 1 small yellow onion, chopped
- 1 tablespoon fresh chopped thyme
- 1 teaspoon garlic powder
- ½ teaspoon smoked paprika
- ½ teaspoon chili powder
- 1 large egg, beaten
- 1/3 cup flour
- 4 sandwich buns, toasted

Instructions:

1. Preheat your grill to medium-high heat and brush the grates with olive oil.
2. Bring the water and quinoa to boil in a saucepan with a pinch of salt.
3. Reduce heat and simmer, covered, for 15 minutes then turn off heat.
4. Place the beans in a mixing bowl and mash them gently with a fork, leaving some of them mostly whole.
5. Stir in the quinoa, onion, corn, and spices until well combined.
6. Add the egg and flour, stirring well, then season with salt and pepper to taste.
7. Divide the mixture into four even-sized patties by hand and brush with olive oil.

8. Place the patties on the grill and cook for 4 to 5 minutes on each side until cooked through.
9. Serve hot on toasted sandwich buns with your favorite burger toppings.

Nutritional Information:

640 calories per serving, 6g fat, 114g carbs, 35.5g protein, 20g fiber, 7g sugar

Asian Black Bean Burgers

Servings: 4

Ingredients:

- 1 ½ cups water
- ¾ cups uncooked quinoa, rinsed well
- 1 tablespoon olive oil
- ½ medium onion, diced
- 1 small carrot, peeled and diced
- 1 stalk celery, diced
- 1 tablespoon minced garlic
- 1 (15-ounce) can black beans, rinsed and drained
- 2 tablespoons smooth peanut butter
- ¼ cup hoisin sauce
- 1 tablespoon soy sauce
- ¼ cup cashews (soaked in water 2 hours)
- 1 tablespoon fresh grated ginger
- 1 teaspoon 5-spice powder
- 4 sandwich buns, toasted

Instructions:

1. Bring the water to boil in a small saucepan then stir in the quinoa and a pinch of salt.
2. Simmer for 20 minutes, covered, until the liquid is absorbed.
3. Turn off heat and fluff the quinoa with a fork.
4. Heat the oil in a large skillet over medium-high heat.
5. Stir in the onion, carrot, celery and garlic – cook for 5 to 6 minutes until tender.
6. Add half of the black beans and cook for another 6 to 7 minutes.
7. Transfer the mixture to a food processor and add 1 cup cooked quinoa.

8. Blend the mixture smooth then add the peanut butter, hoisin, soy sauce, cashews, ginger and 5-spice powder.
9. Blend until smooth and well combined.
10. Transfer the mixture to a bowl and stir in the remaining beans and quinoa.
11. Cover and chill for 30 minutes then shape the mixture into four even-sized patties by hand.
12. Preheat your grill to medium-high heat and brush the grates with olive oil.
13. Place the patties on the grill and cook for 4 to 5 minutes on each side until cooked through.
14. Serve hot on toasted sandwich buns with your favorite burger toppings.

Nutritional Information:

780 calories per serving, 17g fat, 124g carbs, 36g protein, 21g fiber, 12g sugar

Grilled Watermelon Feta Salad

Servings: 4 to 6

Ingredients:

- 1 medium seedless watermelon
- Olive oil, as needed
- 1 large seedless cucumber, sliced thin
- ¼ cup thinly sliced red onion
- 1 tablespoon fresh lime juice
- 1 teaspoon fresh lime zest
- 1 cup crumbled feta cheese

Instructions:

1. Cut the watermelon into 1-inch-thick slices and brush one side with oil.
2. Preheat the grill to high heat and brush the grates with oil.
3. Place the watermelon on the grill and cook for 4 minutes.
4. Remove the watermelon to a cutting board and coarsely chop – transfer to a serving bowl.
5. Toss in the remaining ingredients and serve immediately.

Nutritional Information:

300 calories per serving, 6g fat, 60g carbs, 8.5g protein, 3.5g fiber, 48g sugar

Grilled Corn and Zucchini Salad

Servings: 6 to 8

Ingredients:

- 1 large zucchini, sliced ¼-inch thick
- 1 medium red onion, sliced thick
- ½ cup Italian dressing
- 2 large ears of corn, shucked
- 1 tablespoon olive oil
- Salt and pepper to taste
- 1 teaspoon minced garlic
- 2 to 3 tablespoons fresh lime juice
- ½ cup fresh chopped cilantro

Instructions:

1. Toss the zucchini and red onion with the dressing and let soak for 20 minutes.
2. Preheat your grill to medium high heat and brush the grates with olive oil.
3. Brush the ears of corn with oil and season with salt and pepper to taste.
4. Grill the ears of corn for 8 to 10 minutes then transfer to a cutting board.
5. Place the zucchini and onion on the grill and cook for 4 to 5 minutes on each side until lightly charred.
6. Cut the corn off the cob and coarsely chop the zucchini and onion.
7. Combine the vegetables in a bowl with the garlic then season with salt and pepper to taste.
8. Toss in the lime juice and cilantro to serve.

Nutritional Information:

135 calories per serving, 7g fat, 16g carbs, 2g protein, 1.5g fiber, 5.5g sugar

Grilled Red Potato Blue Cheese Salad

Servings: 6 to 8

Ingredients:

- 3 lbs. red potatoes, cleaned
- 1/3 cup cooking sherry
- ½ cup blue cheese crumbles
- ¼ cup olive oil
- ½ tablespoon Dijon mustard
- ¼ cup diced yellow onion
- Salt and pepper to taste

Instructions:

1. Place the potatoes in a large saucepan and cover with water.
2. Bring to a boil then reduce heat and simmer for 15 to 20 minutes until fork-tender.
3. Drain the potatoes and set aside.
4. Combine the sherry, blue cheese, olive oil, mustard and onion in a small bowl.
5. Preheat the grill to high heat and brush the grates with olive oil.
6. Slice the potatoes thick and brush with olive oil.
7. Season the potatoes with salt and pepper to taste then grill for 5 to 8 minutes until lightly charred, turning once.
8. Place the potatoes in a serving bowl and toss with the dressing to serve.

Nutritional Information:

240 calories per serving, 10g fat, 32g carbs, 5g protein, 3.5g fiber, 2g sugar

Grilled Romaine Blue Cheese Salad

Servings: 8

Ingredients:

- 8 ripe Roma tomatoes, quartered
- ½ cup olive oil
- 2 tablespoons sugar
- 1 tablespoon fresh chopped rosemary
- Salt and pepper to taste
- 2/3 cups sour cream
- ¼ cup blue cheese crumbles
- ¼ cup whole milk
- ¼ cup mayonnaise
- 1 tablespoon red wine vinegar
- 4 romaine hearts

Instructions:

1. Preheat your oven to 225°F.
2. Whisk together ½ cup olive oil, sugar, rosemary, salt and pepper in a bowl.
3. Toss the tomatoes with the dressing then spread them on a rimmed baking sheet.
4. Roast the tomatoes for about 2 ½ hours until tender then set aside.
5. Combine the sour cream, blue cheese, whole milk, and mayonnaise in a mixing bowl.
6. Whisk in the vinegar until smooth – season with salt and pepper to taste.
7. Preheat the grill to high heat and brush the grates with olive oil.
8. Spray the romaine hearts with cooking spray and season with salt and pepper to taste.

9. Grill the romaine hearts for 5 to 10 minutes, turning often, until just charred.
10. Coarsely chop the romaine hearts and toss them with the tomatoes.
11. Serve the salad warm drizzled with the blue cheese dressing.

Nutritional Information:

235 calories per serving, 20g fat, 12g carbs, 3g protein, 2g fiber, 7g sugar

Honey-Dipped Grilled Artichokes

Servings: 4

Ingredients:

- 4 large artichokes, fresh
- 1 lemon, cut in half
- ½ cup tahini sauce
- 1 ½ tablespoons honey
- Salt and pepper to taste

Instructions:

1. Slice about ½ inch off the top of each artichoke then cut them in half vertically.
2. Using a pair of kitchen scissors, cut the pointy ends off the leaves and remove the choke from the center of the artichoke.
3. Rub the lemon over the artichokes, working it in between the leaves.
4. Fill a large saucepan with water and place a steamer insert inside it.
5. Put the artichokes in the steamer and steam for 30 minutes until fork-tender – cool for 15 minutes.
6. Preheat your grill to high heat.
7. Whisk together the tahini, honey, salt and pepper in a mixing bowl.
8. Spritz the artichokes with cooking spray and season with salt and pepper to taste.
9. Place the artichoke halves, cut-side down, on the grill and cook for 4 to 5 minutes until charred.
10. Serve the artichokes hot with the honey dipping sauce.

Nutritional Information:

185 calories per serving, 6g fat, 29g carbs, 7.5g protein, 10g fiber, 8.5g sugar

Garlic Asiago Grilled Asparagus

Servings: 4

Ingredients:

- 1 lbs. fresh asparagus spears, ends trimmed
- 3 to 4 tablespoons olive oil
- 1 tablespoon minced garlic
- ½ cup shaved Asiago cheese
- Salt to taste

Instructions:

1. Preheat your grill to medium heat and lightly oil the grates with olive oil.
2. Place the asparagus in a shallow dish and toss with oil and garlic.
3. Sprinkle the shaved parmesan over the asparagus and season with salt to taste.
4. Place the asparagus on the grill perpendicular to the grates.
5. Grill for 10 minutes then turn the spears – grill another 10 minutes until charred.

Nutritional Information:

175 calories per serving, 15g fat, 5g carbs, 8g protein, 2.5g fiber, 2g sugar

Grilled Avocado with Tomato Salsa

Servings: 4

Salsa Ingredients:

- 2 ripe stem tomatoes, diced
- ½ small green pepper, cored and diced
- ¼ cup diced red onion
- ½ cup fresh chopped cilantro
- ½ teaspoon ground cumin
- Salt and pepper to taste

Avocado Ingredients:

- 2 large ripe avocado
- Olive oil, as needed
- 2 tablespoons fresh lime juice
- Salt and pepper to taste

Instructions:

1. Combine the salsa ingredients in a mixing bowl, stirring well.
2. Preheat the grill to medium heat and lightly grease the grates with olive oil.
3. Cut the avocados in half and remove the pits – leave the skin intact.
4. Brush the cut sides with olive oil and drizzle with fresh lime juice.
5. Place the avocado halves cut-side down on the grill and cook for 2 to 3 minutes until lightly charred.
6. Transfer the avocado halves to a serving dish and fill with tomato salsa.
7. Season with salt and pepper then garnish with fresh chopped cilantro to taste.

Nutritional Information:

230 calories per serving, 20g fat, 14g carbs, 3g protein, 8g fiber

BBQ Stuffed Sweet Peppers

Servings: 4

Ingredients:

- 1 (8-ounce) package cream cheese, room temperature
- 1 cup part-skim ricotta cheese
- 1/3 cup grated parmesan cheese
- Salt and pepper to taste
- 6 poblano chile peppers
- 6 Anaheim peppers
- Olive oil, as needed

Instructions:

1. Stir together the cream cheese, parmesan and ricotta in a small bowl – season with salt and pepper to taste.
2. Preheat your grill to medium-high heat and brush the grates with olive oil.
3. Remove the stems from the peppers and carefully pick out the seeds and membranes.
4. Spoon the cheese mixture into the peppers and toss with olive oil.
5. Place the peppers on the grill and cook for 6 to 7 minutes, turning every minute or two, until the cheese is bubbling.

Nutritional Information:

385 calories per serving, 28g fat, 16g carbs, 19g protein, 4.5g fiber, 3g sugar

Balsamic-Grilled Vegetable Medley

Servings: 8 to 10

Ingredients:

- 3 assorted bell peppers, seeded and quartered
- 2 large Portobello mushroom caps, sliced
- 2 large tomatoes, sliced thick
- 1 large zucchini, sliced on the bias
- 1 large yellow squash, sliced on the bias
- 1 medium eggplant, sliced on the bias
- 1 medium red onion, sliced thick
- ½ cup olive oil
- ½ cup balsamic vinegar, divided
- Salt and pepper to taste

Instructions:

1. Preheat your grill to high heat and brush the grates with olive oil.
2. Combine the vegetables in a large roasting pan.
3. Toss with ½ cup olive oil and ¼ cup balsamic vinegar then season with salt and pepper to taste.
4. Using a pair of tongs, spread the vegetables on the grill, arranging slices perpendicular to the grates.
5. Cook for 2 to 3 minutes on each side until lightly charred.
6. Remove the grilled vegetables back to the roasting pan and toss with the rest of the balsamic vinegar.
7. Season with salt and pepper to taste then serve hot.

Nutritional Information:

170 calories per serving, 13g fat, 13g carbs, 3g protein, 5g fiber, 6.5g sugar

Chipotle Grilled Sweet Potatoes

Servings: 6 to 8

Ingredients:

- 3 lbs. sweet potatoes, rinsed
- 4 tablespoons olive oil
- 1 ½ tablespoons apple cider vinegar
- 1 tablespoon honey
- 1 teaspoon chipotle chili powder
- 1 teaspoon salt

Instructions:

1. Place the sweet potatoes in a large pot and cover with water – salt the water to taste.
2. Bring the water to boil then simmer for 6 to 7 minutes until the sweet potatoes are fork-tender.
3. Drain the sweet potatoes and cool slightly then cut them in half lengthwise.
4. Preheat the grill to medium heat and oil the grates with olive oil.
5. Whisk together the oil, cider vinegar, honey, chipotle chili powder and salt in a small bowl.
6. Brush the cut sides of the sweet potato with the mixture.
7. Place the sweet potatoes cut-side down on the grill and cook for 12 to 15 minutes until lightly grilled and tender.

Nutritional Information:

310 calories per serving, 8.5g fat, 57g carbs, 3g protein, 8g fiber, 3.5g sugar

Grilled Polenta Cakes with Mango Salsa

Servings: 6

Ingredients:

- 6 cups water
- 1 (12-ounce) box polenta
- Salt to taste
- 1 (14-ounce) can corn kernels, drained
- ½ cup grated parmesan cheese
- 1 small red pepper, cored and diced
- Olive oil, as needed
- 2 ripe mangos, pitted and diced
- 1 large tomato, diced
- 2 green onions, sliced thin
- ½ cup fresh chopped cilantro
- 1 large lime, juiced

Instructions:

1. Bring the water to boil in a large saucepan then stir in the polenta.
2. Reduce heat and simmer for 10 minutes, stirring often.
3. Line a baking dish with parchment and set aside.
4. Add the corn, cheese, and red pepper to the polenta and season with salt.
5. Spread the polenta in the parchment-lined dish.
6. Cover the polenta with a sheet of parchment and put a flat baking tray on top.
7. Weigh the tray down with cans to flatten it – chill in the refrigerator for 2 hours.
8. Preheat the grill to medium heat and brush the grates with olive oil.
9. Cut the polenta into wedges and brush both sides with olive oil.

10. Grill the polenta cakes for about 5 minutes on each side until lightly charred.
11. Combine the remaining ingredients in a bowl.
12. Serve the polenta cakes hot with mango salsa.

Nutritional Information:

350 calories per serving, 3g fat, 74g carbs, 10g protein, 5.5g fiber, 15g sugar

Grilled Barbecue Seitan Ribs

Servings: 6 to 8

Ingredients:

- 2 cups vital wheat gluten
- ¼ cup nutritional yeast
- ½ tablespoon onion powder
- 2 teaspoons garlic powder
- 1 ½ tablespoons smoked paprika
- 1 ½ cups vegetable broth
- ¼ cup smooth peanut butter
- 2 tablespoons soy sauce
- 1 ½ teaspoons liquid smoke
- 1 ½ to 2 cups barbecue sauce

Instructions:

1. Preheat your oven to 350°F and grease a square glass baking dish.
2. Combine the nutritional yeast, wheat gluten, onion powder, garlic powder and paprika in a mixing bowl.
3. In a separate bowl, whisk together the vegetable broth, peanut butter, soy sauce, and liquid smoke.
4. Stir the wet ingredients into the dry until it forms a soft dough – knead by hand for 2 to 3 minutes.
5. Spread the mixture in the baking dish, flattening it by hand.
6. Use a sharp knife to slice the mixture into 1-inch pieces then bake for 25 minutes.
7. Preheat your grill to medium heat and brush the grates with olive oil.
8. Remove the seitan ribs from the oven and brush with barbecue sauce.

9. Place the ribs sauce-side down on the grill and cook for 5 minutes.
10. Brush the tops of the ribs with sauce then flip and cook for another 5 minutes until browned.

Nutritional Information:

370 calories per serving, 7g fat, 39g carbs, 40g protein, 3.5g fiber, 18g sugar

Smoked Seitan "Brisket"

Servings: 6

Ingredients:

- 3 cups vital wheat gluten
- ½ cup nutritional yeast
- 2 ¼ cups ice cold water
- 2/3 cups soy sauce
- 2 tablespoons tomato sauce
- 1 tablespoon minced garlic
- 2 teaspoons lemon zest
- 1 tablespoon paprika
- 1 teaspoon chili powder
- ½ teaspoon ground cumin

Spice Mixture Ingredients:

- 5 tablespoons paprika
- 2 tablespoons chili powder
- 2 tablespoons black pepper
- 1 ½ tablespoons sugar
- 1 tablespoon garlic powder
- 1 tablespoon onion powder
- 2 teaspoons cayenne
- 1 teaspoon dry mustard powder

Instructions:

1. Stir together the wheat gluten and nutritional yeast in a mixing bowl.
2. In a separate bowl, whisk together the water, tomato sauce, soy sauce, garlic, and lemon zest.
3. Stir in the paprika, chili powder and cumin then whisk the wet ingredients into the dry.

4. Knead the mixture by hand for about 3 minutes until spongy.
5. Let the mixture rest for 5 minutes then shape into two 8-inch logs – cut each into three pieces.
6. Fill a large pot with water and add the pieces of dough – bring to a boil.
7. Reduce heat and simmer for one hour, turning the pieces occasionally.
8. Turn off the heat and cool for 10 minutes before removing the seitan.
9. Gently squeeze out as much water as you can then wrap in plastic and chill overnight.
10. Start a fire in your smoker and soak the wood chips for about 45 minutes.
11. Rub the seitan pieces with the spice mixture then place the pieces on the grates.
12. Sprinkle some wood chips over the coals and close the smoker lid – smoke for 1 ½ hours, adding soaked wood chips as needed.
13. After the seitan is smoked, brush with barbecue sauce to serve.

Nutritional Information:

375 calories per serving, 4g fat, 34g carbs, 58g protein, 8g fiber, 5.5g sugar

Conclusion

Hopefully after reading this book you have a newfound appreciation for your grill. Why settle for the same old boring barbecue recipes when you can enjoy flavorful dishes like, Grilled Margherita Pizza, and Spicy Asian Grilled Black Bean Burgers? Grilling is not only one of the most versatile grilling methods out there, but it is also incredibly simple. Just fire up the grill and add whatever food you like! If you are ready to give your grill a second chance, pick one of the thirty-five delicious vegetarian BBQ recipes in this book and get cooking!

Printed in Great Britain
by Amazon